Help your friend if he asks for it.

Be able to say, "I'm sorry."

Be helpful.

Share.

Have them over to your house.

Tell them they are good at something.

Let them play in your game.

Help them clean up their room.

Share things—like your lunch.

Compliment them.

Take them places.

Be generous.

Be considerate.

Say, "Good job!"

If you have something you don't want, give it to your friend.

Take turns.

Ways to Be a Friend

Smile.

Talk to your friend.

These ideas were contributed by
Mr. B.'s third grade class,
Derby Academy, fall 1996.

If your friend gets hurt,
bring her to a teacher.

Call them by the names
they want to be called.

Read a word if they can't.

Don't argue.

Play together.

Cooperate.

Respect something your friend does.

When they're upset, comfort them.

If they lose in a game, say,
"Good game!" instead of bragging.

Invite them to play with you.

Try to agree.

Respect their privacy.

If they are discouraged,
cheer them up.

Laurie Krasny Brown and Marc Brown

HOW TO BE A FRIEND

A Guide to Making Friends and Keeping Them

CENTER FOR THE COLLABORATIVE CLASSROOM

For
Maria Modugno

Acknowledgments

Special thanks for their comments and criticism to our
expert readers: Edwin Bartholomew, third grade teacher; Linda Braun,
executive director of Families First Parenting Programs; Dorothy Burlage,
Ph.D., clinical psychologist; Bernie Hawkins, second grade teacher; Phyllis
Oppenheim, special education teacher; Polly Rizzotto, kindergarten teacher;
Judie Stolp, head of lower school; Phyllis Wender, literary agent; and
Denise Yocum, Psy.D., school counselor, Powell Associates.

Center for the Collaborative Classroom
1001 Marina Village Parkway, Suite 110
Alameda, CA 94501
800.666.7270 * fax: 510.464.3670
collaborativeclassroom.org

ISBN 978-1-61003-381-7
Printed in China

7 8 9 10 RRD 20 19

Contents

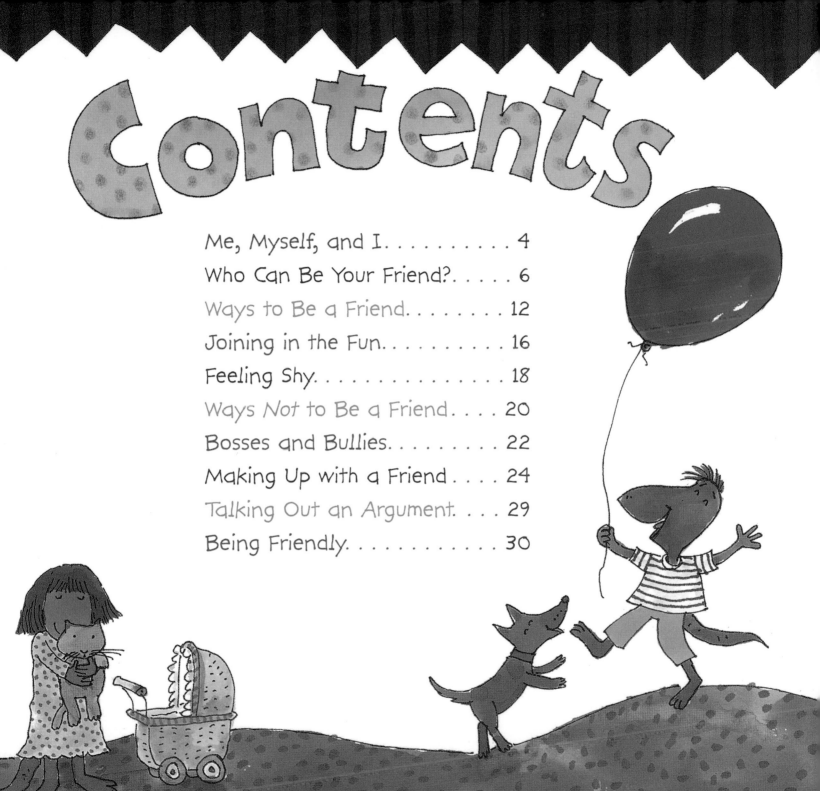

Me, Myself, and I

There are times when it feels good to be by yourself, enjoying your own company.

You can think up ideas, pretend, and play exactly what you want.

With no one else around, you can have all the toys to yourself.

Who Can Be Your Friend?

But some games are too hard to play by yourself. And they're not as much fun all alone.

There are times when you may feel lonely or bored, when you want to have someone to play with.

Anyone who is nice to you and who likes to play with you can become a friend.

Friends can be different from each other in all kinds of ways.

Hi! My name's Martha. What's yours?

My friend is good at the computer.

My baby-sitter is a friend.

My mom would be my friend, except she's already my mom.

He's my boyfriend.

8

But there is one important way
that friends are always alike.

Friends feel the same way about each other!

Ways to Be a Friend

There are many ways to show that you like someone and want to be a friend.

You can play fair. Flip a coin with a friend to see who goes first.

You can protect a friend if someone starts bothering him.

You can share toys and other things.

You can stand up for friends, even when other kids complain about them or make fun of them.

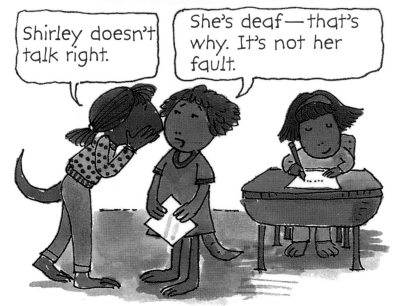

You can invite them to play with you.

You can listen to your friends and pay attention to what they say.

You can try to cheer up a friend who's feeling sad.

You can offer help to friends when they need it.

You can cooperate. Go along with *your friend's* ideas sometimes.

You can compliment your friend, even when she wins and you lose. That's being a good sport.

You can keep your word. Then friends will know that they can trust you.

You can do things for friends, like making them special presents.

Joining in the Fun

Everyone feels left out sometimes. And it's not always easy to join in.

We don't need any more members.

I will too play! Or else . . .

Feeling left out hurts inside. But acting too angry about it usually doesn't help.

Doing nothing isn't much help, either. You may end up feeling helpless and sad.

What you *can* do instead . . . is to invite someone else to play with you.

Want to play?

Or find something you like doing on your own for a while.

Do you guys need a clubhouse flag?

KEEP OUT

ME
O

Cool!

Later, you could try to join in the group again. If you watch to see what they are playing, you might be able to offer some help.

17

When you feel shy, it takes courage even to say hi to someone. But the more you practice, the easier it gets.

19

Ways *Not* to Be a Friend

Friends are bound to disagree about things. Even best friends can bother each other sometimes.

There are many ways to upset your friends.

> No fair! You're cheating!

If you cheat and don't follow the rules.

> You Stupidosaurus!

> Don't call me that!

If you insult them or call them mean names.

> You can't play. It's only for boys!

If you don't let them play.

> Nya, nya— na, na, na!

If you tease or make fun of them.

If you hit or hurt them.

If you don't share things.

If you blame friends for something they didn't do.

If you don't let your friend play with anyone else.

If you act like a poor sport, showing off when you win or quitting so you won't lose.

If you ignore what your friends say.

21

Bosses and Bullies

Being a boss means that you like to tell your friends what to do when you play. You like to make all the rules. But friends may get upset if you never let them have a chance to be in charge.

You be the sister. You be the baby. I'm the mom!

You're always the mom, Annie. I want to decide this time!

Yeah, Annie. Don't be so bossy!

One of the worst ways to treat a friend is to act like a bully and try to scare someone into doing what you want.

If someone bullies you, *try* not to get upset. Tell the bully to leave you alone. Join other, friendly kids. If that doesn't work, ask a grown-up for help.

Making Up with a Friend

There is always more than one way to settle an argument. If you and your friend want to use the same toy, what could you do instead of fighting over it?

When I argue with a friend, Mom says, "Work it out." But how?

Be creative. Think of a way you both can use it.

One minute, five seconds, ten milliseconds left to ride . . .

Decide to take turns.

I'll run home and get my bike.

Okay. I'll go with you.

Try to get enough toys for both of you.

Make a deal. If *you* get what you want, what can your friend have?

If you *let* me ride your bike, I'll *let* you ride my skateboard.

Let's flip a coin to see who rides.

Heads or tails?

Use a trick such as flipping a coin or counting one-potato, two-potato to see who goes first.

I have two race cars. Want to play with them instead?

Okay. Next time I'll bring my bike.

Decide to play with something else.

Arguments

Arguments can make friends feel so angry, they can hardly think about making up . . . at least, not until they find a safe way to get out their anger.

Sometimes an argument just gets worse and worse, angrier and angrier, with no end in sight. Friends may need to separate, take time out, or get some grown-up help.

Talking Out an Argument

Here are some steps to help you talk out an argument:

1 Stop arguing.

2 Calm down. Take deep breaths, count backwards, relax your muscles, or leave the group for a minute.

3 Agree to talk it out.

4 Everyone gets a turn to tell, not yell, their story and be listened to without interruptions.

5 Think up lots of ideas for solving the problem.

6 Try to choose the best solution, the one everyone agrees on and thinks will work.

7 Decide how to go about carrying out this plan.

8 Do it!

9 Remember, arguments are allowed, but meanness is not!

Remember:
In order to please everyone at least a little, you may not get exactly what you want.

Being Friendly

Being friendly means showing that you care about other kids, even the ones you hardly know. You can make them feel important and help them to belong.

It means treating others the way you would like them to treat you!

31

It feels great to have a friend!

Ways Not to Be a Friend

Say, "Ha, ha, you can't do that."

Bite them; push them.

Lie to them.

Boss them around.

Say, "So what?" when they win an award.

Scream.

Call them a name they don't like.

Make mean faces.

Be a poor sport.

Dump them.

Talk behind their backs.

Brag a lot.

Ignore them.

These ideas were contributed by
Mr. B's third grade class,
Derby Academy, fall 1996.

The Center for the Collaborative Classroom (CCC) is a nonprofit organization dedicated to students' growth as critical thinkers who learn from, care for, and respect one another. Since 1980, we have created innovative curricula and provided continuous professional learning that empower teachers to transform classrooms, build school community, and inspire the academic and social growth of children.

Authentic literature is at the heart of our literacy programs. Children's books are deeply interwoven into every lesson, either in a read-aloud or as part of individual student work. Rich, multicultural fiction and nonfiction bring the full range of human experience and knowledge into the classroom, reinforce students' sense of belonging within it, and connect the classroom to the wider world.

Engaged teachers facilitate the exchange of student ideas in collaborative classrooms. These conversations spark curiosity and a desire to participate in the learning process that reap benefits far beyond the immediate goals of learning to read and write. Combining quality curricula and great literature enriches the educational experience for all students and teachers.

We would like to express our thanks to Little, Brown and Company and to Laurie Krasny Brown and Marc Brown for allowing us to reprint this book.